THE ACT OF LETTING GO OF ANGER AND GRIEVE:

A quick guide to a happy and free life.

Daniel C. Nunn

TABLE OF CONTENT

Chapter 1

MEANING OF LETTING GO.

We frequently hear the phrase, “let go”. What do these phrases represent, and is it straightforward to let go?

Psychology, self-improvement, and spiritual traditions talk about letting go and the advantages of accepting it, but what is it?

What Is the Meaning of Letting Go?
Let go meaning:

This word signifies getting rid of unpleasant memories and painful thoughts, toxic impulses, and undesirable behaviors. It also implies cease concentrating on the past or fretting about the future.

Letting go also denotes detachment, the eliminating of attachments to anything that makes you pain or miserable. It signifies the absence of connection, and non-involvement with topics that do not interest you, or which cause you to suffer.

Here is another let go meaning:
It is the act of distancing oneself from unpleasant, pointless, or destructive ideas and sensations. In this process, you release yourself from emotional weight and cease taking things personally. In this process, you eliminate from your life everything that holds you in the past and which does not help you go ahead.

Letting go is the process of liberating oneself from worrying thoughts and painful sensations. This can appear impossible to execute, but with sufficient training and experience, it becomes achievable.

If a given article of clothing is old, tattered, or of no use to you, there is no need to cling to it. You simply go and get a new one.

This should be the same with useless and negative ideas, painful memories and poor habits, unhealthy lifestyles, and even with individuals who make you hurt or sad.

Sometimes, you need to let them go out of your life, and even forget them.

"You cannot sail while the anchor is holding your ship. You need to pull it up. Letting go is like bringing up the anchor of your ship and beginning to sail."

The Negative Effects of not Letting Go

Most individuals are frightened to let go. They are tied to ideas, habits, belongings, and people, and find it difficult to let their needless and destructive attachments free, even if they are causing them to suffer and be miserable.

Anger, bitterness, hatred, and jealousy are like cords that hold you down. You get nothing from them, but you lose a lot by clinging to them. You need to learn to let go of them.

Too much connection with negative individuals demands too much of your time and energy. This participation agitates your thoughts and emotions and generates a loss of tranquility. That's why letting goes of individuals, who make you feel worried and unpeaceful is crucial.

Letting go is crucial for spiritual progress. It is one of the most critical stages toward spiritual enlightenment.

The ego, this creature formed of your ideas and your emotions, beliefs, and habits, does not enable your consciousness to grow higher. It maintains your day-to-day awareness, routines, likes, and dislikes.

To feel a greater awareness, a sense of freedom and enjoyment, you need to ascend beyond your ego. You may do so by letting go of the ideas, emotions, and memories that tie you down and keep you imprisoned inside your ego.

You need to break free of the rope that binds you down like shackles to harmful behaviors, pointless ideas, and unpleasant or sad sensations and memories. You need to sever the connection to them.

Developing the ability to let go may help you achieve that.

When you do not let go, you enable attachment to develop.
When you let go, you enable detachment, freedom, and pleasure to flourish.
Attachment is like an anchor of a ship. Letting go, permits you to raise the anchor, and allow the ship to sail. When no bad ideas, emotions, and behaviors bind you down, you may go on to a better and happier life.

Letting go and disconnect from the sources of misery, provide comfort, pleasure, and inner peace.

Letting go is like moving your head ahead and marching on, instead of being trapped in one spot and continually gazing back.

Letting go is about embracing what is occurring right now and not stressing about what will come up tomorrow. It entails much more than merely declaring you have let go. It's an internal process that must happen for you to feel better and go on with life in a healthy manner.

Chapter 2

HOW TO KNOW WHEN IT'S TIME TO LET GO.

Signs indicating it's time to let go.
To prevent the poisonous explosion of remaining in settings that no longer benefit you, ask yourself whether any of the following 20 symptoms apply.

- When your mind gravitates to memories more than the present.

- When the circumstance gives you more anguish than delight.

- When you anticipate, hope, and urge for the person, place, or circumstance to change.

- When you grow complacent, bored, or resentful.

- When the pattern remains even after you try to change it.

- When you feel alone, unheard, or disregarded.

- When the circumstance is holding you back from developing and becoming who you want to be.

- When you remain, hoping and expecting things to become better.

- When you weep more than you laugh and adore.

- When you feel drained emotionally, spiritually, and physically.

- When you have lost your passion and pleasure.

- When your essential ideas and ideals have changed and you forsake who you are.
- When you cease having fun.
- When you fear this is the best it will be.
- When you force a smile to mask the pain.
- When you lose who you are and stop dreaming.
- When you hold on out of fear of the unknown.
- When you realize you are clinging onto something supposed to be let go.
- When the prospect of getting rid of the circumstance seems spacious.

- When you believe in a better life for yourself.

This list serves as a caring guide to help you make the appropriate option for you. If you find yourself replying yes to the bulk of these questions, it may be time for you to let go and take a step forward. Trust your future and trust you will be directed to happiness.

Chapter 3

REASONS WE SHOULD LET GO.

If you're able to let go and start accepting things as they are instead of how you'd want them to be, you'll discover that you'll suffer less from the difficulties of stress, emotional links to the past or future, dissatisfaction with others, struggles with loss, and succumbing to fear.

Letting rid of previous habits can help you open your mind to new lifestyles as well as fresh thoughts and outlooks. As you evolve, your viewpoint will change as well. Let go of old thinking and move forward to meet your goals.

Emotional advantages of letting go

There are substantial psychological advantages of letting go. When we let go of uncomfortable emotions and concentrate on the present moment this controls our sentiments more efficiently. There is strong evidence that mindfulness meditation improves both mental and physical health. Mindfulness also strengthens our resilience to cope with unfavorable life experiences.

We are all conditioned to perceive the world through specific lenses. Via our childhood, youth, and early adulthood we build certain ways of perceiving the world through our experiences. These experiences become glasses through which we make meaning of new events and individuals we encounter. In many aspects, our brains are conditioned to search for parallels to construct a shortcut via which we can judge new experiences to guarantee that we learn from the past. The trouble with this is that over time we become less able to take in information that is different from our established ways of perceiving the world since this creates too much worry.

Many years ago psychologists created a hypothesis referred to as 'cognitive dissonance' which refers to 'the sense of unpleasant tension which arises from having two competing concepts in the mind at the same time. To provide an example of this, if through time and terrible life experiences I believe that 'I am not good enough when I accomplish in some area of my life this is likely to generate dissonance since it doesn't mesh with my vision of myself. To escape this feeling of painful conflict I could then justify my accomplishment as good luck or tend to minimize how much of my success has to do with my real ability. Essentially our brains are driven to make sense of things in a manner that is comfortable to us to avoid a sensation of anxiety even if the familiar ideas are detrimental to us. We cling on to the past to prevent the prospect of future suffering yet by holding on we frequently end up enduring much worse anguish because we don't expose ourselves to new possibilities.

Letting go entails stepping back from an unpleasant experience and noting what is going on in our head, examining our thoughts and sensations. Over time the capacity to monitor our mind implies that we might acquire a certain curiosity about our experiences rather than consider our ideas and sensations to be 'the truth. When we are coping with a painful event such as a loss of a relationship we could be challenged to let go since our mind is continually reliving the experience and attempting to comprehend it which can often result in rumination. Letting go entails noting where our mind is going, how it is pulled to specific unpleasant ideas, emotions, or memories again and again, and focussing on the current now. This involves both acceptance of what we think and feel but also a conscious effort to refocus our awareness on another experience; the place we try to redirect our mind to could be 'internal' such as our breath or 'external', for example, the sounds in a room or a conversation we are having with a friend. Our mind could then return the unpleasant ideas and sensations again and again thus letting go isn't always an objective that is attained fast but a process that we continually have to engage with over a lengthy period.

Chapter 4

THE NEGATIVES EFFECTS OF NOT LETTING GO.

When you build up every recollection of things that went wrong, how you were injured, how you harmed others, what you lost (emotionally, physically, financially, socially, legally, etc.), and so on, it's a bit like putting too much weight to a cart or overpacking the trunk. At some point, you'll overtax the system and it will break, unable to carry the burden. Bad memories are like that – they're just too much weight to bear. The fact that you allow them to accumulate means they aren't being dealt with. They're going to remain in your consciousness (or the back of your mind, if you've shoved them out of your immediate thoughts) until you do, all the while creating even more problems than you want or need.

Physical Consequences

Stress-related physical conditions are one of the most immediate effects of not letting go of what's troubling you. You're overworked, trying to deal with the mountain of bills caused by the addict (or you, if you are the addict) (or you, if you are the addict). You find that you can't sleep through the night. You lose your appetite and start shedding pounds at a precipitous (and unwanted) rate. Your looks begin to degrade.

You have a migraine and other headaches, physical aches and pains, and are prone to coughs, colds, and infections. Some folks who do not cope with all the harmful ideas in their head acquire significant or chronic disorders. Hypertension, heart attack and stroke, and various kinds of cancer may be induced by chronic and unresolved stress, a process called stacking. Muscle tightness in the form of a stiff neck, shoulders, and lower back discomfort may frequently be connected to stress. Ulcers and rheumatoid arthritis are two other physical diseases that might come from unresolved stress – or not dealing with your unpleasant thoughts.

Emotional Consequences

Plagued by anxiety and insecurity, you frequently run unpleasant scenarios through your thoughts.

What if I lose my home, my possessions?
What if I can't pay my bills and my car is repossessed?
How can I trust the addict, my spouse/significant other/child/sibling/parent/family member/friend - the person with whom I've spent so much time, energy, commitment, and love?
What will happen to our/my children? How will I ever be able to face our/my friends again?
The outcome of all this mental anguish may be disastrous. Suddenly, you discover you

don't trust anybody, neither the addict nor yourself. You may resort to snooping, following the individual, going through his or her belongings, reading their mail or other correspondence, or calling strange phone numbers that appear on the monthly home or cell phone bill. It doesn't matter what form of addiction is present, whether it's for alcohol, street or prescription drugs, compulsive sexual activity, compulsive gambling, compulsive spending, or even overwork — once your emotional roller-coaster begins going, it's hard to stop. One thing is certain: if you keep up the pace, you'll either wind up in a wreck or fly off the rails, figuratively speaking.

Not Being Good Enough

Of all the bricks we might hurl at ourselves, one of the most hurtful is the negative idea that we are simply not good enough. Again, it's immaterial whether you are the addict or the spouse/partner/family member/friend who has similar ideas. What occurs is that you will do and say everything to make yourself more worthy in the eyes of the other. But whatever you try doesn't seem good enough. Somehow, all you do is fail. You can see it in his or her eyes, that wordless accusation, the turning away. What happens next? You beat yourself up even more for your inability to meet up to the expectations you imagine the other person has – or, maybe has already verbalized. None of this is productive. All of it is an additional illustration of the harmful ramifications of not letting go.

Being Drawn to the Wrong People

All this bad energy that's self-directed has other implications as well. Not only are we unable to move on when we're distracted by the trainwreck of our ideas, but we find ourselves attracted to precisely the wrong sorts of individuals. It may feel comfortable to surround ourselves with people that seem familiar, that seem just like us, but ask yourself what it is about that person or persons that makes you want to be around them. If you are a co-dependent — the enabler of an addict, you are likely attracted to those who mimic the most important connections in your history – those of your parents. That's probably what helped you locate the connection in your present relationship with the addict. Or, if you are the addict who has trouble letting go of all those negative thoughts, you most likely chose someone who will allow you to continue in your self-destructive behavior. In either case, the relationships you choose are not healthy. Whether you are the addict or the loved one/friend, etc. of the addict, you need to select healthier relationships. One way to do that is to concentrate first on healing yourself. Of course, if you are married to the individual, this doesn't mean that you necessarily have to walk away from the relationship – at least, not immediately. What you eventually decide to do should be based on mutual agreement and a choice that's in the best interest of both. Letting go of the past – especially a past strewn with the litter of poor choices – can be incredibly difficult and painful for everyone involved.

Reinforcement of Negative Behavior

Let's consider a situation that may or may not appear familiar. It is, however, illustrative of the negative effects of not letting go. A woman, we'll call her Barbara, has been married to Phil for 20 years. They have two teenage children, a girl, 17, and a boy, 14. Phil has been an alcoholic for most of his adult life (he's now 45). Barbara is 40, now overweight by about 30 pounds, a non-stop smoker, and a habitual complainer. Phil recently lost his job due to his alcoholism. Now, the couple has no health insurance for the family, and Barbara needs a hip replacement. In pain, she's been downing street drugs her daughter got from a boyfriend and now has an addiction to the painkillers. Adding to the misery, Barbara caught Phil cheating on her with a neighbor and good friend. Phil swears he won't see the woman again, but Barbara is convinced that Phil's been unfaithful for many years, citing unexplained expenses, strange phone numbers, and long absences from home. Their children hear explosive arguments, sometimes resulting in physical violence. The daughter has been smoking marijuana for the past two years as the tension at home has gotten increasingly worse. Furthermore, she thinks she may be pregnant since she's had unprotected sex with her boyfriend and has missed her last two periods. The son has started failing in school, is becoming a loner, and sneaks his sister's joints from her purse. This family is clearly in crisis. None of them are attending to the mountain of baggage that their actions have piled up in their minds. They each blame the other for their troubles. Barbara fosters Phil's drunkenness while compensating through overeating. Once she suspected (and then knew about) Phil's infidelity, Barbara's rage boiled over.

She took illegal drugs even though she knew it was dangerous and against the law. She blames Phil for the family's dire financial circumstances, along with her emotional state. The children, seeing the mess of their parent's lives, have begun a downward spiral of their own. Thus, negative thoughts and actions have perpetuated and spilled over into a reinforcement of negative behavior. Until all these family members get professional help and/or start attending counseling or 12-step self-help groups, the situation will continue to get worse.

Chapter 5

HOW TO LET GO AND BE HAPPY.

Take deep breaths
In the excitement of the moment, it's easy to neglect your breathing. But that type of shallow breathing you do when you're upset maintains you in fight-or-flight mode.

To overcome this, consider taking calm, controlled breaths you inhale from your abdomen rather than your chest. This helps your body to rapidly settle itself.

You may also carry this breathing practice in your back pocket:

Find a chair or spot where you can comfortably sit, allowing your neck and shoulders to relax.
Breathe deeply through your nose, and pay attention to your stomach rising.
Exhale through your mouth.

Try completing this exercise 3 times a day for 5 to 10 minutes or as required.

Recite a reassuring mantra

Repeating a soothing phrase might make it easier to express tough emotions, like anger and irritation.

Try softly repeating, "Take it easy," or "Everything's going to be okay," the next time you're feeling overwhelmed by a circumstance. You can do this out loud if you wish, but you can also say it under your breath or in your brain.

You may also have a list of words on your phone for a fast reminder before a tough work presentation or hard meeting.

Try visualizing

Finding your happy spot in the middle of a flight delay or business setback might help you feel more comfortable in the moment.

When grappling with boiling stress, try drawing a mental image to calm your body and brain:

Think about a real or fictional area that makes you feel joyful, serene, and secure. This may be that camping trip to the mountains you took last year or an exotic beach you'd want to visit someday.
Focus on the sensory aspects by visualizing yourself there. What are the scents, sights, and sounds?

Be conscious of your breathing and retain this picture in your mind until you feel your worry start to lift.
Mindfully move your body.
Sometimes, sitting motionless might make you feel even more nervous or on edge. Mindfully moving your body with yoga and other soothing movements helps alleviate tension in your muscles.

The next time you're presented with a stressful circumstance, consider taking a stroll or maybe performing some light dancing to distract your mind from the tension.

Check your viewpoint

Moments of intense stress may skew your perspective of reality, making you feel like the world is out to get you. The next time you feel the rage boiling up, attempt to evaluate your viewpoint.

Everyone has terrible days from time to time, and tomorrow will be a new start.

Express your displeasure

Angry outbursts won't do you any favors, but that doesn't mean you can't express your anger to a trusted friend or family member after a particularly unpleasant day. Plus, letting yourself have room to express some of your anger stops it from building up within.

Defuse rage with comedy

Finding comedy on a tense occasion might help you preserve a balanced viewpoint. This doesn't mean you should just laugh off your difficulties, but looking at things more lightly might assist.

The next time you feel your fury boiling up, contemplate how this circumstance could seem to an outsider. How would this be humorous to them?

By not taking oneself too seriously, you'll have more opportunities to recognize how inconsequential tiny annoyances are in the broader scheme of things.

Change your environment

Give yourself a break by taking some personal time from your immediate surroundings.

If your house is messy and stresses you out, for example, take a trip or a lengthy stroll. You'll likely discover that you're more able to sift through the clutter when you return.

Recognize triggers and find alternatives

If your daily commute transforms you into a ball of fury and irritation, consider choosing an alternate route or leaving early for work. Got a noisy co-worker that regularly taps their foot? Look into some noise-canceling headphones.

The objective is to discover and comprehend the factors that trigger your rage. Once you're more aware of what they are, you may take efforts to prevent falling victim to them.

If you aren't sure where your anger is coming from, try to remind yourself to take a minute the next time you feel furious. Use this time to take stock of what transpired in the minutes preceding your thoughts of rage. Were you with a certain person? What were you doing? How were your sentiments building up to that moment?

Focus on what you appreciate

While concentrating on your day's tragedies might feel like the natural thing to do, it won't benefit you in the short or long run.

Instead, try focussing on the things that went well. If you can't find the silver lining in the day, you might also try considering how things might've gone much worse.

Seek assistance

It's entirely natural and good to feel irritated a furious from time to time. But if you can't shake a poor mood or continuously feel overwhelmed by rage, it may be time to seek assistance.

If your anger is harming your relationships and well-being, consulting with a trained therapist may help you work through the roots of your anger and help you create stronger coping mechanisms.

Regardless of what leads you to feel furious, it's how you address it that counts most.

But what happens when anger takes over and you can't find a means to confront and release these feelings?

When this happens, the consequence is what professionals generally refer to as pent-up fury, or anger that's been suppressed and not released. This form of rage might impact your mental and physical health. That's why it's crucial to recognize, acknowledge, and move beyond these sentiments.

Causes

If you've ever experienced prior rage or been around someone who is coping with it, you may be wondering what causes these severe sentiments that can take over your body and mind.

Symptoms

The first step in coping with pent-up rage is knowing how to identify when it's occurring.

"If you're holding onto anger, you may find yourself playing it out with others, frequently strangers, or with people where you can easily get away with it," This effect is a normal self-defense strategy termed displacement. An example is road rage when maybe the true problem is that you're upset with your job. Other symptoms to watch out for include:

bad sleep\sfeeling on edge
becoming upset easily\sbecoming frustrated and irritated in little conditions

criticizing or harming others

Treatment

Recognizing and recognizing that you have pent-up rage is a huge step toward coping with it.

Challenge your thoughts

When coping with anger, psychologists typically utilize a process called cognitive restructuring that teaches you to replace negative beliefs with more logical ones.

This mental shift helps you calm down your thoughts, tap into reasoning, and, eventually, turn your demands into requests.

Practice relaxation exercises

If you can learn to slow down and practice deep breathing, you're more likely to release some of the anger you're feeling.

Use creative arts

One approach to learning how to control anger healthily is via a creative art outlet. Bash noted that often frequently, music, painting, dance, or writing may be fantastic instruments to convey feelings that might be tough or powerful.

The bottom line

Anger is a frequent aspect of existence. It's regarded as a fully normal human feeling. But if you find yourself feeling angry regularly, particularly over previous incidents, you must work through these emotions and forgive yourself and others for what occurred.

Sometimes, understanding how to accomplish this might be tough. That's why being able to recognize the reasons and then knowing how to deal with them healthily is a critical technique for reducing pent-up rage.

Chapter 6

KEY FACTS TO NOTE ABOUT LETTING GO.

1. Strive to be more conscious of your thoughts

It could sound unusual to you, yet frequently, we let ideas run through the mind without giving them careful attention. We frequently allow these ideas to impact how we feel and behave.

You need to endeavor to be conscious of the things you think, about and regularly, ask yourself if they are essential and valuable to you. If they are not required and helpful, refuse to contemplate them and have anything to do with them.

2. Shift your focus to pleasant ideas

If you realize that you regularly think negative ideas or concentrate on challenges and anxieties, consider changing your focus to cheerful thoughts so that the negative ones lose their influence over you.

If you do so frequently, in time, you would be able to reject the negative ideas and rid yourself of them.

3. Strive to be more conscious of your moods and emotions

In the same manner, as with your ideas, strive to be more conscious of your feelings and emotions, and avoid unpleasant angry, and resentful ones.

You also need to be watchful, and not let the bad feelings others convey to you, movies you see, or the news you read, impact negatively how you feel.

When becoming aware of unpleasant sentiments, anger and resentment, anxiety and fear, ask yourself if they are beneficial to you in any way. Do you derive any advantage from them?

You do not need to cling to them. Trade them for pleasant emotions.

4. Make peace with yourself and other people

Discover how to concentrate your attention

Learn about emotional detachment and letting go

Make peace with yourself and with other people. Anger, anger, resentment, and grudges are futile.

It may not be simple to get rid of them, but when you continuously think about the suffering that they are bringing you, you will finally cease allowing yourself to wallow in them.

5. Don’t linger on the past

Stop focusing on the past. With practice, you will finally be able to do so.

It is futile to dwell in the past. You cannot bring it back, and if the past was awful, why replay it in your mind?

Living in the past is like putting an anchor in a perilous sea, where there is heavy weather. It is a not required thing to accomplish.

6. Don't take things personally

Stop taking things personally. Not everything people say is about you. You can be perceiving what they say erroneously, they might be simply kidding, or what they say is unimportant.

You need to establish some self-esteem and inner strength, and stop letting people's comments and opinions affect you. This has been addressed in depth in the book, "Emotional Detachment for Happier Life", referenced below.

"When you choose to let go of unfavorable past experiences, not to obsess yourself with concerns and anxieties, and to demonstrate emotional detachment toward them, you choose happiness."

www.ingramcontent.com/pod-product-compliance
Lightning Source LLC
LaVergne TN
LVHW020527160826
845677LV00015B/3936

* 9 7 9 8 3 5 2 3 9 8 0 4 3 *